D1221040

WITHDRAWN

3 1192 00475 8734

769.92 Maill.A
Maillol, Aristide,
The woodcuts of Aristide Maillol
:

DATE DUE

MAY 1 - 1998

MAR 2 5 2000

NOV 2 6 2004

DEMCO, INC. 38-2931

THE WOODCUTS OF
ARISTIDE MAILLOL

A COMPLETE CATALOGUE WITH
176 ILLUSTRATIONS
EDITED BY JOHN REWALD

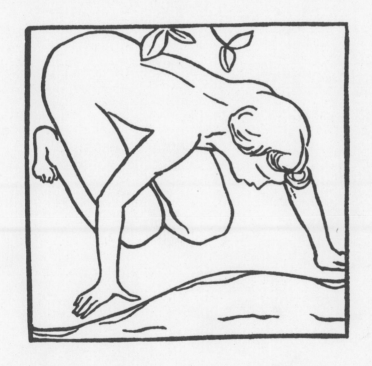

NORTH SUBURBAN LIBRARY SYSTEM

PANTHEON BOOKS INC · NEW YORK

1951

COPYRIGHT 1943 BY PANTHEON BOOKS INC.
41 WASHINGTON SQUARE, NEW YORK

INTRODUCTION

THE WOODCUTS OF ARISTIDE MAILLOL

ARISTIDE MAILLOL: SELF-PORTRAIT
CUT ON WOOD BY G. AUBERT

During the nineteenth century, etching was not always very popular among artists, and woodcutting, oldest of the graphic techniques, was even less popular, while lithography, which had just been invented, immediately found enthusiastic supporters. This can be explained to some extent by the nature of the graphic processes involved. Each of the three graphic techniques, the relief, the intaglio and the planographic process, offers very different artistic possibilities, yields dissimilar results and requires special modes of execution.

In the planographic or lithographic process the artist simply makes his drawing with a special lithographic crayon, either directly on stone or on paper, and the proofs can be pulled by any printer. Thus artists can obtain without any special effort almost unlimited editions of their drawings.

The intaglio or etching process, on the other hand, obliges the artist who is anxious to exploit all the possibilities of the technique to etch and print his plates himself. In etching the plates, sometimes in several acid baths, in using drypoint or in combining these two processes, he has to be patient and extremely skilful. His proofs will be satisfactory only if he pulls them himself, since proper inking often determines the character of the work. Hence the complicated manipulation of the metal plate was left, during the last century, to artists like Meryon or Bresdin, who restricted themselves to etching. While most of the nineteenth-century painters made few and comparatively unimportant etchings, there were, at the close of that century, artists like Degas, Mary Cassatt, Pissarro and Whistler who devoted much time and great gifts to this medium, but their etchings, especially those of Degas and Pissarro, were long ignored by the public.

The relief process, to which woodcutting belongs, may be said, in so far as the execution is concerned, to offer the advantages and problems of both lithography and etching. Some artists, like Constantin Guys, were content to make their drawing on the woodblock or on paper, leaving the actual cutting to specialized engravers. Rouault today follows this procedure. But if the artist goes to the trouble of cutting his own drawing, he has to devote much time, skill and even physical effort to the completion of his work. And he may have to print his blocks himself, if he wants to obtain those special effects that characterize the woodcuts of Gauguin, Munch or—among contemporary artists—Bernard Reder.

It is obvious that the popularity with artists of these three graphic techniques is based on the attractiveness of the very different kinds of prints each has to offer and on what may be called the "economy" of their execution. Naturally, each of these processes requires a different conception and a different style, but the artist who masters these processes must also decide through which one of them he can best realize his aims. He knows that each of the three processes is rich in possibilities, but if he is unable to devote considerable time to his work, he must renounce the black velvety lines of the woodcut or the etching's limitless scale of precise strokes. Daumier's caricatures for the *Charivari* were possible only because lithography enabled him to have his drawings printed at almost the very moment he completed them. It takes hours merely to cut a wood-block, and to etch a metal plate may take days. Besides, lithography, the simplest graphic process, also demands the least experience and offers the artist greater

BURNE-JONES: WOODCUT ILLUSTRATION FROM THE
KELMSCOTT CHAUCER, 1896

control of output. Whereas the etcher has to contend with the haz-
ards of the acid bath which may bite the lines deeper into the plate
than he desires, and whereas a drawing cut on wood by someone
other than the artist loses almost automatically some of its original
qualities, the lithographic drawing does not undergo any changes
when drawn directly on the stone and suffers only minor changes
when transferred to it. So it is easy to understand why lithography
was preferred to the woodcut, which, as an art medium, was almost
completely defunct during the last century. Woodcuts were used only
for illustrating popular books and magazines; finally this function
was taken over by photomechanical processes.

Curiously enough, the graphic arts persisted after the invention of
photography and the different techniques of reproduction based on
it; they even underwent a revival which culminated in many portfolios of prints and in a series of illustrated books of enduring fame.
The growing vulgarization of images of all kinds seems to have

Chapter II. Evil tidings come to hand at Cleveland...

NOT long had he worked ere he heard the sound of horse-hoofs once more, and he looked not up, but said to himself, "It is but the lads bringing back the teams from the acres, and riding fast and driving hard for joy of heart and in wantonness of youth" But the sound grew nearer and he looked up and saw over the turf wall of the garth the

WILLIAM MORRIS AND WALTER CRANE: PAGE FROM
THE GLITTERING PLAIN, KELMSCOTT PRESS, 1894

stimulated the taste of artists for the ancient handicraft of book-printing. This revival of the graphic arts at the end of the last century had its roots in England and France. While the French put more emphasis on lithography, adapted it to posters and book illustrations, and made experiments in color-printed lithographs and etchings, the British turned their attention to illustrative woodcuts and to typography. Both movements achieved a high degree of technical perfection; the French, however, accused the British of lacking artistic invention and originality, while the latter replied that "there does not seem to be any feeling amongst the French designers for the artistic value of lettering, or any serious attempt to cultivate better

viii

HERO AND LEANDER BY
CHRISTOPHER MARLOWE
AND
GEORGE CHAPMAN

Hero's description and her love's;
The fane of Venus where he moves
His worthy love-suit, and attains;
Whose bliss the wrath of Fates restrains
For Cupid's grace to Mercury:
Which tale the author doth imply.

CHARLES RICKETTS: TITLE-PAGE FROM HERO AND LEANDER,
VALE PRESS, 1894

forms."[1] This rivalry found its expression in works which bear the
mark of rare taste and conscientiousness and of seldom equaled
workmanship.

It was William Morris, the English poet, who led the way in the
revival of the illustrated book. In a period of artistic uncertainty, he
chose the Gothic style as a model, and if his books seem sometimes
too faithful to this model, they have nevertheless the great merit of
being a first step towards a new understanding of the handicraft of
book-making. Already in 1866 Morris began to cut on wood the
drawings of his friend Burne Jones, to be used as book illustrations.
Twenty-five years later he founded the Kelmscott Press, which is re-

WOODCUT ILLUSTRATION FROM THE
HYPNEROTOMACHIA POLIPHILI, 1499

sponsible for some of the most representative publications of that period. But the mixture of Gothic and Pre-Raphaelite inspiration gives these works a sentimentality and artificiality which is far from the decorativeness of the real Gothic. However, these attempts stimulated new conceptions of book-making and induced many artists of the younger generation to try their hand at this art.

Because of the efforts of William Morris, book-making again became an art. Illustrations and text, paper and type, page-arrangement and binding, were no longer considered separately. Their carefully planned harmony, as well as the fact that the type-setting and the printing were done by hand, made this kind of book the legitimate successor to the first great publications after Gutenberg's invention. This however did not convince some critics.

"The claims to excellence," wrote Veblen in 1899, "put forward by the later products of the book-maker's industry rest in some meas-

WOODCUT ILLUSTRATION FROM THE
HYPNEROTOMACHIA POLIPHILI, 1499

ure on the degree of its approximation to the crudities of the time
when the work of book-making was a doubtful struggle with re-
fractory materials carried on by means of insufficient appliances.
These products, since they require hand labor, are more expensive;
they are also less convenient for use than books turned out with a
view to serviceability alone; they therefore argue ability on the part
of the purchaser to consume freely, as well as ability to waste time
and effort. It is on this basis that the printers of today are returning to
'old-style,' and other more or less obsolete styles of type which are
less legible and give a cruder appearance to the page than the 'modern' . . . The Kelmscott Press reduced the matter to an absurdity."[2]

Obviously these considerations not only ignore the artistic qualities of the Kelmscott books but also misrepresent the problems faced
by the early printers. For it should not be forgotten that the original
book-makers were highly skilled and rich in many experiences which

xi

RICKETTS AND SHANNON: WOODCUT ILLUSTRATION FROM
DAPHNIS AND CHLOE, 1893

have since been lost. And it is also true that any work executed by hand represents in its inevitable imperfection and irregularity a certain emotional value which the machine product lacks. William Morris' merit lies precisely in the fact that he emphasized skill and workmanship at a time when the enthusiasm for mechanics was leading to a dangerous confusion between "perfection" and art. With him the book again became what it had been in the beginning, a beautiful object designed to delight the eye as well as the mind.

Valid objections to Morris' ventures cannot come from those who criticize from the point of view of mass-production and "modernity," but only from those who speak from the standpoint of artistic

RICKETTS AND SHANNON: WOODCUT ILLUSTRATION FROM
DAPHNIS AND CHLOE, 1893

worth. This question, neglected by Veblen, preoccupied Camille
Pissarro, whose views of Morris' enterprise still hold. "I do not
doubt that Morris' books are as beautiful as Gothic art," he wrote,
"but it must not be forgotten that the Gothic artists were *inventors*
and we have to perform, not better, which is impossible, but differ-
ently and following our own bent."[3]

Charles Ricketts, Charles Shannon and their young French friend,
Lucien Pissarro, tried to adapt artistic book-making to their own
time, each striving to create a personal style. Unlike Morris, who
was not a creative draftsman, they engraved their drawings themselves, and Ricketts even designed borders, initials and several

founts of type which he cut. While Lucien Pissarro, under the influence of his father, strove for a simple rustic style in black and white, his English comrades did not wholly free themselves from Morris' style. Abandoning the Gothics, however, they turned to the early Florentine and Venetian printers. They particularly admired the linear beauty and decorative character of the *Hypnerotomachia Poliphili.*

In 1893, Ricketts, together with his friend Shannon, illustrated and printed Thornley's translation of *Daphnis and Chloe.* So close was the collaboration of the two artists that it is impossible to distinguish the work of one from that of the other, especially since they sometimes both worked on the same block. Their woodcuts emphasize the "most sweet" character of the text. The charm of the illustrations lies in the ornamental stylization and rather sentimental conception, but they show at the same time a capitulation to the monotony and mannerism so often to be found in English art of that period. Like Morris' publications, their book combines noble conceptions with a lack of inspiration.

From 1889 on, Ricketts and Shannon had been publishing *The Dial* at their Vale Press—though very irregularly. Their magazine was devoted to the revival of the woodcut drawn and cut by the artist and "printed from the wood to ensure the greater sweetness of the printing." Their efforts were directed against the photomechanical line-cut that made it unnecessary to engrave line drawings on wood. As a matter of fact, Aubrey Beardsley had shown to good effect that black and white compositions could easily be reproduced by this mechanical device. Thus the perfection of printing techniques seemed to endanger the very ideals which Morris and his pupils had devoted so much research, skill and labor to defend.

When, in 1896, Walter Crane, collaborator with William Morris, termed black and white the "most vital and really popular form of art at the present day,"[4] this statement was certainly an exaggeration, at least in so far as the woodcut was concerned. In France, where the efforts of the English were largely unknown, a great many periodicals dedicated to the graphic arts sprang up during the mid-nineties. Most of them did not last very long. They were interested almost exclusively in lithography; only *l'Image*[5] (1895), edited by Beltrand and Lepère, and the short-lived *Ymagier* (1894–95), which was devoted to the "images d'Epinal" and works by artists from the Pont-Aven group led by Gauguin, paid special attention to woodcuts and wood-engravings.

At that time many artists in France were attracted by the wood-block—the wood-engraver Lepère is the most famous of these—but interest seldom went with talent. While lithography inspired the daring experiments in line and color of Chéret and Lautrec, who in turn were followed by Bonnard, while Degas, Pissarro and Mary Cassatt exploited the etching to the full, the woodcut had made no important progress since the days of Doré. Camille Pissarro, introduced to the English movement by his son, was tempted by the wood-block, but was able to devote little time to it, and his few efforts remained completely unknown. Reacting against the mystic tendencies of the Pre-Raphaelites who dominated English art, Pissarro tried to put into the woodcut his sincere feeling for nature, deliberately avoiding mannerisms and facile effects. He began by drawing on wood a series of pastoral scenes for a portfolio entitled *Travaux des Champs*, which was never completed; he also did some illustrations for *Daphnis and Chloe*, but, not having nude models, he had to discontinue them. The few drawings on wood by Pissarro that were cut by his son Lucien are distinguished by the harmonious disposition of blacks and whites and the simplicity and poetry which is the main quality of the painter's entire work. His prints have a healthy naïveté and are most unlike the elaborate English and French woodcuts inspired by the cult of the archaic.

But Pissarro's woodcuts, familiar only to a few friends, could hardly play a role in the development of the art. It was Gauguin who, despite or perhaps because of his lack of familiarity with the graphic arts, poured the explosive power of his imagination and will into the ancient craft. With complete disregard for all traditional approaches, and taking no account of the English movement, he attacked the woodcut from a new angle, turning his attention to the wood itself. Morris, Ricketts and Shannon for all their emphasis on workmanship had really made pen drawings cut on wood, but Gauguin conceived his designs in terms of the wood itself—they could only exist on wood, receiving their character from the block and the engraver's tools. Adventurous and experimental, Gauguin showed a remarkable feeling for the specific traits and possibilities of his material. Had he not already expressed himself in oil paint, clay, pastel, marble and ceramics? Renouncing the elaborate finish which distinguishes the cuts of Morris and his followers, Gauguin hid behind a wilfully rough execution the most precious refinements of conception and style.

Gauguin did not fail to find in this graphic technique new ways of expressing his very personal talent. The influence his woodcuts have exerted derives as much from the new attitude as from the new technique. Gauguin's wonderful gift for simplification, his intuitive feeling for the decorative line, his clear delight in playing with forms, his European sensitiveness and "barbaric" execution, all are completely expressed in his woodcuts.[6]

Among the young artists who at the beginning of their careers were influenced by Gauguin, only one was able to develop a personal style in woodcutting. This was Aristide Maillol, who owes to Gauguin his freedom from conventional conceptions and his feeling for ornamental arrangements.

Maillol began as a painter in the Ecole des Beaux-Arts in Paris. With the best will in the world he was unable to find in the official teaching any sustenance for the capacities he sensed, however vaguely, within him. Then, around 1888, he was struck by several paintings of Gauguin; these opened new horizons to the beginner and inspired him to new ardors. However, he did not concentrate on painting but on an art which he had studied in the Paris museums, namely tapestry. It is interesting to note that several years before, in 1883, Gauguin himself had thought of making tapestries, an idea which he later abandoned, although he actually tried his hand at various applied arts, ceramics and glass-painting for example. Certainly Gauguin must have followed with interest the efforts of the young artist who in 1892 exhibited his first large tapestry, *Music*, a work Gauguin greatly admired and praised.

This first tapestry of Maillol, like those which were to follow it, is clearly indebted to Gauguin in conception, arrangement and choice of colors. Emphasis is placed on the line which encircles extremely simplified forms despoiled of their plasticity, reduced to pure ornamentation and showing the first signs of the stylization that was to lead to *l'Art Nouveau*.

Along with these tapestries Maillol executed a few lithographs, most of which were conceived as studies for his woven works. At the same period he also made several woodcuts which mark the stages of his development from his first faltering efforts to his contact with Gauguin. A portrait of his aunt (1) and a scene from Hero and Leander (2), both very carefully done, still show the painter's concern to express on wood a multiplicity of nuances and details. Figures and background interpenetrate and are drowned in heavy shading. But soon the first nudes (3 and 4) testify to the development of a more truly graphic conception for blacks and whites, the forms become harmonized and the lines take on an ornamental character. And by the time Maillol finished *The Wave* (5) and *The Sea* (6), two compositions which he had carried out in painting and in tapestry, he had completely assimilated the experiments of Gauguin; he contented himself, however, with black and white, and did not depend upon color, stencils, wiped ink, in short the whole bag of tricks used with such success by Gauguin.[7]

Around 1900 a sudden weakening of his sight forced Maillol to give up tapestry-making forever, and it seemed that he had renounced the graphic arts too, for during the next ten years he devoted himself exclusively to sculpture. In this medium also, Maillol showed in his first works the influence of Gauguin, but finally achieved a mastery which owes nothing to the art of the exotic, a naïve purity, sobriety, grace and serenity which are found in the masters of antiquity.

It was for his sculpture that Maillol began to be known; his first woodcuts and lithographs had attracted so little attention that his name does not even appear in the standard works on the graphic arts published before 1925. While Maillol was working with clay and stone, his friends, particularly Maurice Denis and Pierre Bonnard, were devoting much of their time to lithography, and Maillol's dealer, Ambroise Vollard, was publishing works which marked an entirely new period in the history of the illustrated book. The first of the publications was Verlaine's *Parallelement* illustrated by Bonnard, who surrounded the verses with delicate sketches, delightful, fantastic drawings, which overflow the margins, insinuate themselves between the lines and fill whole pages with whimsical charm. The second volume illustrated by Bonnard, and published shortly afterwards, in 1902, by Vollard, was *Daphnis et Chloé*. This pas-

LUCIEN PISSARRO: WOODCUT ILLUSTRATION FROM
LA BELLE AU BOIS DORMANT, ABOUT 1895

toral had a special appeal for painters, many of whom have tried their hand at representing the idyllic images which abound in the text. But this time Bonnard adopted another mode of presentation, the text and the illustrations are clearly separated, each page is divided, the upper part, two thirds of the page, bears the drawing in rectangular format, while several lines of text fill the lower part of the page. The illustrations of Bonnard, lithographs as in his first volume, have the freshness of sketches cast lightly on the paper and, far from encumbering the text, they are like mirrors in which are reflected the fields and the herds, the trees and the streams, the flowers and the two lovers celebrated by Longus.

The conception of this book follows the principles set forth by Maurice Denis, who, as early as 1890, had declared: "When the plastic character [of the illustration] is in conflict with the typog-

CAMILLE PISSARRO: ILLUSTRATION FOR DAPHNIS AND CHLOE
CUT ON WOOD BY LUCIEN PISSARRO, ABOUT 1893

raphy, you have a monstrosity. . . . The illustration is the decoration of a book, it does not mean placing black photographic squares on the white spaces or on the writing, it does not mean naturalistic slashes placed at random in the text, or other unstudied cuts, pure expressions of manual cleverness, often imitated from the Japanese. We should find this decoration without being enslaved by the text, without making the subject of the drawing correspond exactly to that of the writing; what we want is rather an embroidery of arabesques on the pages, the accompaniment of expressive lines."[8]

And some years later, Charles Shannon and Lucien Pissarro had proclaimed that the illustration should add to the book "an element of visible poetry."[9]

Maillol was to think of all this and of the *mise en page* employed by Bonnard when, around 1910, he for the first time attempted book illustration. The credit for having interested the artist in this field must go to Count Kessler. Struck by the classical character of Maillol's statuettes, he invited the sculptor in 1908 to travel with him to Greece. It was during this trip that the book on which Maillol and his patron were to collaborate was conceived.

"His wishes at once coincided with mine," Kessler later wrote, "when I told him about my project to found a press and publish books created entirely from the standpoint that illustration and typography should form a unity, instead of remaining formally unrelated, running along parallel lines, as in most of the illustrated books of modern times. This unity could be achieved if the illustrations sprang from the letter type, the monumental, simple, not bizarre but nevertheless formally rich letter type, which can bear monumental, simple, yet subtle illustrations. I thought I had found such a letter type in the works of the Italian book-printers of the 15th century. . . . We agreed on a letter type of the great Venetian printer Jenson; the type was monumental yet not archaic, it was winged with inner tension, and it gleamed with tender light. I had this type recut. Maillol also insisted that every page of paper be as finely wrought as a rich carpet. After many attempts on Holland, German and English hand-made paper, then on Chinese and Japanese paper, had failed to satisfy him, we founded our own little laboratory and later a factory in Monval near Marly, where, with the collaboration of Maillol's nephew Gaspard, after many attempts, we were able to produce a new paper which satisfied Maillol's requirements. Or rather we manufactured several types of paper, one of which, composed mainly of Chinese raw silk, was especially strong and fine, but also very expensive."[10]

Maillol and Kessler chose Virgil's *Eclogues* as the text to be illustrated. According to Kessler, "as soon as the decision was made, drawing after drawing seemed to sprout in Maillol's sketch books, they came apparently without effort on his part . . . . And then all these drawings incorporated themselves just as effortlessly in the typography; he cut them with a view to the *mise en page*, for his invention cannot create other than decoratively, that is in terms of the relation of his work to the setting for which it is made."[11]

Maillol had carved his first sculptures on wood and it is not surprising that he chose the woodcut rather than the lithograph for his illustrations. He knew the medium and he had the necessary skill; besides, the woodcut can be brought into much more natural and intimate accord with the typography than can the lithograph, especially as both can be printed at the same time. Bonnard, in choosing lithography, had had exactly the opposite purpose in view, that is to say, the separation of text and illustration, which he further emphasized by using a grey or even a colored ink for the lithographs while the text was in black type. Thus Bonnard's images seem less forward than the typography; light and discreet, they are almost like marginal sketches. Maillol, on the other hand, wanted to incorporate his illustrations in the text itself and embed them in the typography in the manner attempted by William Morris. He even went to the length of first printing the text page by page so as to create illustrations in accord with it, and, in addition to cutting the wood himself, actually supervised the making of the paper. However, the style of his illustrations was completely opposed to the archaisms and mystic tendencies of the English publisher. Maillol, too, had studied the woodcuts of the fifteenth century, admiring their masterful naïveté, the resonant black lines, the plastic contours, the simplicity of means employed and the ornamental character of the compositions; his preference went to simple, rustic, sometimes even gauche images— like those of the *Aesop* printed in Ulm, or the *Buch der Natur* from Augsburg, and especially French woodcuts of that period—and if his own prints are like theirs, it is not because he imitated them, but because he, too, was able to combine simplicity and serenity with an exquisite sensibility.

In addition to medieval books, Maillol also studied Japanese and Chinese prints to complete his understanding of the *mise en page*, the organization of the space, delicacy of detail and simplification of forms. Freeing himself from the almost brutal influence of Gauguin, Maillol discovered that the line can be more than an arabesque, that it can suggest forms. Then, too, he brought to his graphic medium not only his early experience but also unique predispositions: the decorative conception of the former designer of tapestries and the plastic feeling of the sculptor. The line, henceforth, was much more than an ornament for him, it was the limit of the three-dimensional bodies which he evoked with an absolute economy of means. And Maillol brought still another quality to his illustrations, a direct and inti-

PAUL GAUGUIN: MARURU, WOODCUT, ABOUT 1894

mate sentiment for nature which guided his hand and stimulated
him to recreate what his eyes had seen.

Maillol is not an "inventive" illustrator able to ornament any
kind of text. His imagination never leaves the realm of things seen;
it might even be said that the inspiration for his illustrations derives
not from the text but from the memories which the reading of the
text evokes in him. For this reason he has chosen to illustrate only
those texts which—ancient or modern—call to mind images of rustic
life or of love. In fact, Maillol finds models for his illustrations in
his immediate environment, a section of France which for cen-
turies has preserved an austere, pastoral simplicity. At Banyuls,
where he was born, at the foot of the Pyrenees, in an Arcadian countryside of wine-growers and fishermen, he contemplates the shepherds and the young girls, the lambs and the hares, the mountains,
the sea and the vegetation. Thus for his illustrations of the *Eclogues*,
the *Contrapas*, an old Catalonian dance which goes back to the ancient Greeks who once colonized this region, inspired the dance of
the Woodland Nymphs (26), the design for the funeral mound (27)

PAUL GAUGUIN: AUTI TE PAPE, WOODCUT, ABOUT 1894

was suggested by an old monument near Banyuls, and the fountain
of Galatea (47) by a fountain in Maillol's country place. Again he
gave Silenus (29) the features of his intimate friend, the painter Ter-
rus, and to Silvanus (49) those of Auguste Rodin. These instances
show that if Maillol created images in harmony with the printed
page, the text and the typography, he nevertheless did not turn his
back on truth and spontaneity—he was inspired by life and not by
history.

Begun in 1912, the production of this book was interrupted by
the war and was not taken up again until 1925; it was concluded in
the following year. The book was printed under the direction of
Emery Walker who had been William Morris' master printer.
Count Kessler, intending to follow it with the *Georgics* also illustrated by Maillol, entitled it, VERGILIUS MARO: THE EC-
LOGUES AND GEORGICS; VOL. I: THE ECLOGUES, but
the second volume was never begun, and Maillol did not return
to the project until ten years later, just before Kessler died.

In Virgil's *Eclogues*, printed after so much research and hard

ARISTIDE MAILLOL: WASHERWOMAN, LITHOGRAPH, ABOUT 1893

work—efforts completely sublimated by its perfect beauty—Maillol
appears as one of the foremost illustrators of the twentieth century.
The artist himself, greatly satisfied by the noble aspect of the book,
acquired a taste for illustration and never again abandoned his engraver's tools even though sculpture continued to absorb him. He
constantly fills his sketchbooks with drawings, scenes caught on the
quick, immediate observations, loving studies of plants and animals.
His pencil catches people at work and surprises the attitudes of wine-
growers, of women gathering herbs and peasants laboring in their
fields. He turns his attention to the fig and almond trees, transcribing
their fragile branches, their leaves, flowers and fruit. Often his eye
follows the movement of hares, which he loves best of all the animals, and many pages of his notebooks show these creatures in their
characteristically graceful and whimsical attitudes. Afterwards, in
his studio, Maillol goes over his notebooks, to emphasize a line here,
to eliminate another there, until simple and rounded forms emerge.
When he finally transposes them on wood, he obtains with an absolute economy of means—black, flexible lines which encircle the forms

ARISTIDE MAILLOL: MUSIC, DESIGN FOR A TAPESTRY,
LITHOGRAPH, ABOUT 1892

and suggest their fullness—the maximum effect. He never tries to imitate in the engraving the character of a drawing, his aim, on the contrary, is to release the full flavor of his subject through an austere and deliberately simplified representation of it. He tries to sum up in a few sober lines living forms and gestures, while careful to organize these in harmonious and decorative compositions. He is able to express the purity of things seen and to stress their poetry by means of a simple black line. These lines with which he evokes his subjects have their own life, they have an innate grace, they vibrate and sing, they are at once naive and suave, chaste and sensual.

The second work illustrated by Maillol appeared in 1931. This, *Belle Chair*, by Verhaeren, is accompanied—except for three ornaments cut on wood—only by lithographs, while the third book, Ovid's *Ars Amandi*, combines the two techniques. Twelve full page lithographs of nudes, interpolated in and without direct relation to the text, alternate with woodcuts which enliven the text pages. These woodcuts are in a freer style, they have more flowing lines than the rugged illustrations for the *Eclogues*.[12] While they lack the intimacy and charm of the latter, they are well suited to Ovid's text. Their elegance does not prevent certain compositions from attaining a supreme beauty, especially those in which the stonecutter's hand is most clearly evident. Pasiphae and the White Steer (59) or Long Caress (65) seem graven with the chisel and have an almost miraculous plasticity.

However, it was only in *Daphnis and Chloe* that Maillol again found a text which inspired him. This idyll of two divinely beautiful beings, stirred by sensual shame and innocent voluptuousness, this story of two children in whom gracious nature kindled a pure and carnal love, Maillol set without hesitation in his native country. It was the daughters of wine-growers, the sons of fishermen, the hares of his neighbors, that appeared before the artist's eyes as he read Longus. And he not only read, he lived the story of Daphnis and Chloe, he saw it unfold each time he walked in the vineyards or along the shores of the Mediterranean. An immense joy filled him when he rendered the episodes of the story, a joy which vibrates in his woodcuts and completes the poetry of the pastoral that has inspired so many illustrators. Maillol does not consider his woodcuts illustrations: they are to him images which are part of the text and express in signs the sentiments evoked by the story-teller's words, as if the author and the illustrator had conceived the work together.[13] To achieve the unity of text and engravings, Maillol chose a presentation less austere than in the Virgil book. The illustrations are scattered freely across the pages, and for the English edition, the printer Philippe Gonin (a Swiss book-maker who devotes himself to publications of Maillol) adopted a brownish grey ink for the illustrations, so as to separate text and images in the same way as in Bonnard's *Daphnis et Chloé*. But the French edition, which appeared shortly afterwards, simplified the printing by using the same black ink for both.

It is significant that for his illustrations of *Daphnis and Chloe*, Maillol selected undramatic episodes, or when this was not possible, reduced the dramatic content. What interested him was the love of the two children, a love which earth and sky, mountains and sea seemed to imitate. Maillol does not care for the dramatic capture of Daphnis and only shows his tender reunion with Chloe (84), while the brutal carrying off of the young girl is represented merely by a woodcut showing a Methymnaean carrying her in his arms (96), and the turbulence accompanying her return is not illustrated at all. Similarly the poetic episode of the pursuit of Syrinx only inspired Maillol to make a cut which represents the body of a young girl disappearing into the reeds (100). And the scene in which Daphnis climbs to the top of a tree to pick the last apple for Chloe, a scene whose audacity Ricketts and Shannon dealt with fully, is summed up for Maillol by the moment in which Daphnis gives the fruit to his betrothed (111). In the same spirit he reduces the splendor of the grape-gatherings to the sports of a loving couple in the vines (87), and, instead of representing the feasts celebrating the reunion of Daphnis and Chloe with their parents, simply shows Chloe given to her lover (122). Thus Maillol extracts all the "sweetness" of the pastoral, without encumbering himself with archaeological details in the representation of rustic life of more than a thousand years ago. What inspires him in this text is precisely that element which makes it true for all eternity: the awakening of passionate love in the setting of a peaceful countryside.

It so happens that we have the early drafts and the first conceptions of the *Daphnis and Chloe* woodcuts—these are the only woodcuts of Maillol of which the first states are known. It is true that most of these "states" simply show the woodcut with the background not yet blocked out, but in some instances the engravings were really reworked, largely to refine the lines, after the first proofs had been pulled. The original conceptions are sometimes almost indistinguishable from the final cuts, but in general the composition adopted shows, compared to the first conception, a tendency towards simplification; shades are indicated with greater economy of means (76-77), details have been suppressed (112-113) or added (101-102), lines are more balanced (124-125). In some cases the first conception had to be rejected because of errors in the cut, as with the knapsack of Daphnis (91) or the foreground interrupted by a white line (116). But the definitive woodcut is never greatly different from the first conception, perhaps because the artist completely formulates his image before he cuts it on the wood block.

If love is the theme of the illustrations for *Daphnis and Chloe*, this is doubly true of the woodcuts Maillol did for a collection of

WOODCUT ILLUSTRATION FROM THE AESOP PUBLISHED IN
VERONA, 1479

Verlaine's poems, *Chansons pour Elle*. These woodcuts, which, incidentally, may have been executed before the *Daphnis and Chloe* illustrations, are devoted wholly to carnal joy, a subject dear to Maillol, which he has also celebrated in a series of etchings done to illustrate Ronsard's *Folastreries*, which Vollard proposed to publish, but never did.

The illustrations Maillol executed for Verlaine's *Chansons pour Elle* are very different from his other woodcuts. Intended to go with verses, they do not blend with the typography but accompany each poem like tail-pieces. They are lively and whimsical sketches whose

WOODCUT ILLUSTRATION FROM KONRAD VON MEGENSBURG'S
BUCH DER NATUR, AUGSBURG, 1475

character is clearly inspired by the wanton verses of the poet. They have nothing of the classical inspiration and lyricism of the illustrations for Virgil and Longus. Nevertheless, they represent an equally characteristic side of Maillol's art; the dry wit of the peasant and the sensitive sensuality of the sculptor are perfectly expressed in these illustrations. It is no secret that Maillol has always been interested in bodies lovingly interlocked, his little notebooks are full of curious sketches which represent every aspect of love-play; these sketches are, of course, not intended for publication. It goes without saying that terms like "obscene" or "pornographic" have no rela-

WOODCUT ILLUSTRATION FROM L'ABUSE EN COURT, LYON,
ABOUT 1480

tion to these studies, for they were not made with a view to excit-
ing specific emotions. Maillol's erotic drawings—like those of all
true artists—simply represent the will to give artistic expression to the
most human of all subjects. If Maillol likes to consider himself an
inheritor of the eighteenth century, it is in part because he shares the
unashamed and lofty eroticism of Boucher, Watteau, Fragonard and
many others.

Maillol selected from the "licentious" drawings in his sketchbooks those closest in spirit to Verlaine's poems, and he executed a
number of additional studies especially for the volume. These graceful, lively, spirited woodcuts have a naive malice and a rough joy-
ousness comparable with certain medieval images. It is no accident
that Maillol was attracted by Ronsard's *Folastreries;* except for
Frans Masereel and Bernard Reder, only Maillol—among contemporary artists—could illustrate the verses of Master François Villon,
or the *Droll Tales* of Balzac.

However, Maillol has chosen not to illustrate works of this kind.
On the contrary, he has recently returned to the project—originally

WOODCUT ILLUSTRATION FROM THE AESOP OF JOHANN ZAINER,
ULM, 1475

conceived with Count Kessler—of illustrating Virgil's *Georgics*.
Philippe Gonin hopes to publish these in two volumes with a hundred woodcuts. Here Maillol has again found a pretext for render-
ing the environment familiar to him from birth, that part of south-
ern France to which he is attached by reverent piety and by some
profound artistic sympathy. His great admiration for Virgil may be
explained by the fact that, at Banyuls, Maillol feels so close—if not in
time, then in space—to the Latin poet, observing all about him the
very same beings, plants and objects that appear in Virgil's verses.

Maillol's notebooks are again filling with drawings for illustrations. These are, in the main, sketches of trees, of all the trees in the
neighborhood, from the cypress and acanthus to the humble fig-tree
which Virgil left out; they describe sometimes groups of trees, a
single tree in all its aspects, or even a lonely branch, a few leaves and
a fruit organized in a decorative composition which reminds one of
Japanese prints. Then there are the plants, the ears of wheat and the
vines, and finally there are the animals. Noteworthy among the latter are the studies of hares, creatures whose entire grace Maillol

xxxi

catches with special delight. Finally there are studies of the work in the fields, of men and women digging, picking fruits, gathering herbs, furrowing the soil. Some of these drawings are done with great care, and worked over several times, but others seem to have been achieved at the first try. All these sketches are made from nature and then cut on the woodblock.

The tired eyes of the aged artist are not up to the task of engraving the drawings and he had to be resigned to relegating this fatiguing work to others. But the cuts are made under his strict supervision, and the aesthetic requirements of Maillol are too high for him to permit the slightest departure from his drawings. The woodcuts which are to illustrate the *Georgics* will be perfect expressions of his creative will. Did not Holbein and many of the old masters who never cut their works themselves achieve their complete expression in this medium?

Maillol hopes to illustrate the *Odes* of Horace when he finishes his woodcuts for the *Georgics*, for if his hands are often too tired now to hold the sculptor's or engraver's tools, he nonetheless never stops drawing and continually searches for those simple and harmonious lines that are the glory of his woodcuts. The engraved work of Maillol is thus not yet finished, although it has already enough richness, variety and finality to justify this catalogue.

The woodcuts Maillol will add to the long list presented here can only add to his renown as an illustrator. He belongs with Bonnard, Rouault, Picasso and all those who—in our time—have taxed their ingenuity to decorate the printed page. But he also occupies a place apart, for he alone has realized in a traditional yet modern style the complete harmony of typography and woodcut, while almost all the contemporary illustrators have preferred lithography, etching, aquatint and even line-cuts to the wood-block, and have seldom collaborated in the organization of the printed page. The books illustrated by Maillol are the ultimate fruit of that renaissance of the printer's art proposed almost a hundred years ago by William Morris. However, the woodcuts of Maillol are more than a new page in the history of one of the noblest among the applied arts, they exist in their own right, separately from the lettering, forming a world of tender lines and simple forms which communicate the artist's sense of beauty.

With his tapestries, sculptures and drawings, Maillol's woodcuts are an inexhaustible source of happiness.

The mood they inspire is best suggested by Swinburne's line:

I wist not what, saving one word—Delight.

WOODCUT AFTER A DRAWING BY ARISTIDE MAILLOL,
PUBLISHED IN L'IMAGE, 1896

NOTES

1. W. Crane: *Decorative Illustration*, London, 1896, p. 268

2. T. Veblen: *The Theory of the Leisure Class*, London, 1899, p.162

3. C. Pissarro: *Letters to His Son Lucien* (August 19, 1898), New York, 1943

4. W. Crane: *Decorative Illustration*, London, 1896, p. 208

5. It was in *l'Image* that a woodcut from a drawing of Maillol appeared in 1896. See the reproduction on page xxxiii

6. In a hitherto unpublished letter to Ambroise Vollard, Gauguin wrote, concerning his lithographs and woodcuts: "En cette matière, comme toute autre, je ne cherche et ne trouve la perfection de facture." (Tahiti, April 1897)

7. See L.G.Cann: The Engraved Work of Maillol. *The Arts*, New York, October 1928

8. M. Denis: *Théories*, 1890–1910, Paris, 1912, p. 10

9. C. Ricketts et L. Pissarro: *De la typographie et de l'harmonie de la page imprimée—William Morris et son influence sur les arts et métiers*, London, 1898, p. 17

10. H. Kessler: Warum Maillol Vergils Eklogen illustriert hat. *Querschnitt*, Berlin, November 1928

11. *idem*

12. See A. Hentzen: Buch-Illustrationen von Aristide Maillol. *Philobiblon*, Brünn, 1938, Heft 1

13. See J. Rewald: Les bois gravés d'Aristide Maillol, *Marianne*, Paris, September 14, 1938

CATALOGUE OF ARISTIDE MAILLOL'S WOODCUTS

The editor and the publisher wish to express their gratitude to Jean Goriany, Karl Nierendorf, Carl O. Schniewind, Heinz Schultz, Erhard Weyhe, George Wittenborn and Mrs. Walter Weil who were most helpful in gathering the material for this catalogue.

CATALOGUE OF ARISTIDE MAILLOL'S WOODCUTS

Unless otherwise mentioned, the woodcuts are reproduced in their original size, and their dimensions are therefore not listed in this catalogue. Only signatures cut in the block are mentioned here, and no reference is made to hand signatures. It may be said, however, that all the prints published by Petiet in Paris are signed M in pencil by the artist, while the numbering is not in his hand.

WOODCUTS EXECUTED BETWEEN 1893 AND 1900

1. THE ARTIST'S AUNT, [LA FEMME A LA JARRE]. The signature AM in the lower right corner is separated from the composition. A few unnumbered proofs were published by Petiet.

2. HERO AND LEANDER. 6 x 6⅞ in. (15.2 : 17.5 cm.). Signed near lower margin, to right of center. 60 numbered proofs published by Petiet; 10 on Japanese paper and 50 on Chinese paper. [Reduced]

3. RECLINING WOMAN. 3⅟₁₆ x 8¾ in. (7.8 : 22.3 cm.). Signed M in the upper right corner. 75 numbered proofs published by Petiet; 15 on Japanese paper and 60 on Chinese paper. [Reduced]

4. RECLINING NUDE. 4⁹⁄₁₆ x 13⁷⁄₁₆ in. (11.6 : 34.1 cm.). Unsigned. A few unnumbered proofs were published by Petiet. [Reduced]

5. THE WAVE. 6¹¹⁄₁₆ x 7¹¹⁄₁₆ in. (17 : 19.5 cm.). Signed AM in the lower right corner. 60 numbered proofs published by Petiet; 10 on Japanese paper and 50 on Chinese paper. The subject and composition of this woodcut correspond to a painting done about 1898 (H. de Monfreid coll.) and to a tapestry executed about 1902 (Prince A. Bibesco coll.). See Rewald: Maillol, plates 33 and 41. [Reduced]

6. THE SEA. Size unknown. Reproduced by P. Camo: Aristide Maillol, Paris, 1926, p. 12 (erroneously called a *drawing*). The subject and composition of this woodcut correspond to a painting executed about 1895 (Petit Palais, Paris). See Rewald: Maillol, plate 65. [Reduced]

7. EVE AND THE SNAKE. Size unknown. According to L. G. Cann: The Engraved Work of Maillol, *The Arts*, Oct. 1928, this woodcut was published by Petiet and proofs are very rare. [*Not reproduced*]

PUBLIUS VERGILIUS MARO: ECLOGAE

PRINTED at the Cranach Press, Weimar, of Count Harry Kessler, who planned the volume. Aristide Maillol designed and himself cut on wood forty-three illustrations for the volume so planned, during the years 1912–14 and in 1925 at Banyuls in the Pyrenees. Eric Gill cut the title page and all the initial letters. The ornament of these letters was designed and cut by Maillol. Edward Prince cut the punches for the type, under the supervision of Emery Walker. The roman type was cut after that used in Venice by Nicolas Jenson in 1473. The italic type was designed by Edward Jonston. The paper was made by a hand-process (devised in joint research by Count Kessler and Aristide and Gaspard Maillol) by Gaspard Maillol, in a workshop set up for this purpose at Monval near Marly, France. Printing of the German edition was begun on the hand-presses of the Cranach Press at Weimar early in 1914. The work was interrupted by the war, and resumed in June 1925.

The German edition (translation by Rudolf Alexander Schröder) consists of eight copies on vellum, marked A to H, of which the copies marked F to H are not for sale; thirty-six copies on the "silk-paper" invented by Count Kessler and A. and G. Maillol, numbered I to XXXVI, of which XXVI to XXXVI are not for sale; two hundred and sixty copies on hand-made paper of pure hemp fibre and linen, numbered 1 to 250, of which 226 to 250 are not for sale.

The French edition (translation by Marc Lafargue), published in 1926, has only six copies on vellum. The numbering of the other copies is the same as in the German edition.

The English edition (translation by J. H. Mason), published in 1927, consists of six copies on vellum, marked A to F, of which five only are for sale; thirty-three copies on imperial Japanese paper, numbered I to XXXIII, of which XXVI to XXXIII are not for sale; two hundred and twenty-five copies on hand-made paper of pure hemp fibre and linen, numbered 1 to 225, of which 201 to 225 are not for sale.

All the copies printed on vellum are accompanied by three extra sets of Maillol's woodcuts: one set with the illustrations printed in dark brown on vellum, one set with the illustrations printed in black on yellow paper and one set with the illustrations printed in red on white Chinese paper. All the copies numbered in Roman numerals are accompanied by an extra set of Maillol's woodcuts, printed in black on white paper. One print of each set usually is signed in pencil with Maillol's initial. Some of the copies numbered in Arabic numerals are accompanied by one single signed woodcut.

The size of the books (and the accompanying sets) varies between 12 x 8½ inches and 13¼ x 10¼ inches.

The page indications correspond to the German edition. Where the English edition differs from the German, the page on which the illustration is reproduced in the English edition is given in brackets.

EIGHTH ECLOGUE

NINTH ECLOGUE

TENTH ECLOGUE

S. INITIAL B, p. 65 English edition only

T. INITIAL G, p. 97 English edition only

U. INITIAL D, p. 103 English edition only

V. INITIAL J, p. 65 German edition only

W. INITIAL M, p. 45

X. INITIAL V, cover (see No. 8 of this catalogue)

According to L. G. Cann: The Engraved Work of Maillol, *The Arts*, Oct. 1928, Maillol executed 50 woodcuts as illustrations for Vergil's Eclogues, 43 of which are reproduced in the book. Only one of the seven rejected cuts is known and can be listed here:

53. A SHEPHERD PLAYING ON HIS PIPE. Signed *M* in the lower right corner. 75 numbered copies published by Petiet; 15 on Japanese paper and 60 on Chinese paper.

Q. HORATIUS FLACCUS: CARMINA

WITH one woodcut on the title page by Aristide Maillol. Planned for the Cranach Press by Count Harry Kessler but never published.

54. FAUN AND NYMPH, TITLE PAGE. Size unknown. Reproduced after *Philobiblon*, Jahrgang 10, Heft 6, p. 226.

EMILE VERHAEREN: BELLE CHAIR

ELEVEN unpublished poems by Emile Verhaeren with eleven lithographs and three woodcuts by Aristide Maillol. Published in 1931 by Edition d'Art Edouard Pelletan, Helleu et Sergent, Paris. The edition consists of one hundred and twenty-five copies; the copies numbered 1 to 5 are on *vieux Japon Pelletan*, the copies numbered 6 to 25 are on *Japon à la forme*, the copies numbered 26 to 75 are on *Monval à la cuve*, and the copies numbered 76 to 225 are on *vergé de Hollande*. There are also thirty "gift-copies" numbered in Roman numerals. Size of the book 11¼ x 9½.

55. STANDING NUDE, TITLE PAGE

56A. INITIAL C, p. 39

B. ORNAMENT, on the cover and on p. 37

OVIDE: L'ART D'AIMER

WITH fifteen woodcuts and twelve lithographs by Aristide Maillol. French translation by Henry Borneque. Published by Philippe Gonin in Paris, 1935. The edition consists of two hundred and seventy-five copies: two hundred and twenty-five copies numbered 1 to 225, of which twenty-five are not for sale, and fifty copies numbered I to L, printed for A. Zwemmer in London, of which twenty-five are not for sale. All the copies are printed on hand-made paper of pure hemp fibre, manufactured by Canson and Montgolfier according to Aristide and Gaspard Maillol's formula. The size of the book is 15¼ x 11⅜. Since the woodcuts are not closely related to any special episode in the text (with the exception of number 59) the titles here listed were invented.

57. NUDE WAVING HER HAIR, TITLE PAGE

FIRST BOOK
58. NUDE ASLEEP, p. 13 (3 x 6⅝ in.) (7.7 : 16.7 cm.) [Reduced]
59. PASIPHAE AND THE WHITE STEER, p. 21 (5 1/16 x 6½ in.) (12.9 : 16.5 cm.) [Reduced]
60. ABANDON, p. 29 (3 3/16 x 6 9/16 in.) (8 : 16.7 cm.) [Reduced]

SECOND BOOK
61. LOVERS UNDER A TREE, p. 57 (3 x 6⅝ in.) (7.7 : 16.7 cm.) [Reduced]
62. DREAMING NUDE, p. 65 and on the cover
63. LEDA, p. 81

THIRD BOOK
64. THE KISS, p. 97
65. LONG CARESS, p. 109
66. EMBRACE, p. 122
67. BOY WITH A STAG, colophon
68A. INITIAL S, p. 5
  B. INITIAL C, p. 44 and 124
  C. INITIAL J, p. 82

LONGUS: DAPHNIS AND CHLOE

"A MOST SWEET, and Pleasant Pastorall Romance for Young Ladies, translated out of the Greek of Longus by Geo. Thornley."

Edition of two hundred and fifty copies, numbered and signed, printed on hand-made paper manufactured by an old process rediscovered by Aristide Maillol. With woodcut illustrations drawn and engraved by Aristide Maillol. Printed by Philippe Gonin on his hand-press in Paris for A. Zwemmer in London; finished on December 7, 1937.

The French edition (translation by Amyot, revised and completed by P.-L. Courier), consists of five hundred copies on *papier Maillol*, numbered 1 to 500, and some copies numbered in Roman numerals which are not for sale. (However, there have been some French copies with Roman numbers and marked H. C., accompanied by an extra set of 20 proofs, on the market.) Printed and published by Philippe Gonin in Paris; finished on December 7, 1937, but issued only in 1938.

The English edition, size 7¹³⁄₁₆ x 5⅛ is bound in vellum. The woodcuts are printed in brownish grey while the text is printed in black. The French edition is not bound, size 8⅝ x 5⅝. Woodcuts and text are printed in black.

There is an unnumbered edition of just the woodcuts in a small portfolio 8 x 5¼, entitled "Daphnis et Chloe, Bois originaux d'Aristide Maillol." These portfolios contain 49 woodcuts printed either in red or black on white paper. Some portfolios with 56 woodcuts contain also the first conceptions for the illustrations and a certain number of woodcuts in their first state. These first-state proofs show the woodcut with background not yet blocked out.

The portfolio with the illustrations for *Daphnis and Chloe* contains first states, with the background not yet blocked out, of the woodcuts here catalogued under numbers 69, 74, 79, 82, 85, 86, 87, 89, 92, 95, 96, 99, 103, 106, 109, 110, 111, 114, 118, 119, 120, 121, 126.

In the following woodcuts the black line framing the composition is not part of the wood-block (its size differs in the English and

French editions): 71, 72, 74, 79, 89, 92, 95, 103, 110, 114, 115, 121, 122.

The number of illustrations executed by Maillol and actually used in the book (without counting the initials) is 46 woodcuts. However the English edition contains 52 woodcut illustrations, and the French 48, since some of the groups of three goats have been separated and the animals reproduced on different pages.

The page indications in the following list correspond to the English edition. Where the French edition differs from the English edition, the page on which the illustration is reproduced in the French edition is given between brackets.

69. CHLOE BATHING, COVER OF THE FRENCH EDITION. In the English edition this woodcut appears on p. 135.

70. DAPHNIS AND CHLOE, TITLE PAGE and p. 188 of the English edition.

FIRST BOOK

71. THREE GOATS, English edition p. 11. The two upper goats appear also on p. 147, and the lower goat on p. 208 of the English edition.

72. THREE GOATS, French edition p. 11

73. TWO NYMPHS DANCING, first conception

74. TWO NYMPHS DANCING, p. 15 [14]

75. DAPHNIS AND CHLOE PICKING FLOWERS, p. 20

76. DAPHNIS PLAYING HIS PIPE FOR CHLOE, first conception

77. DAPHNIS PLAYING HIS PIPE FOR CHLOE, p. 22 [23]

78. CHLOE WASHING DAPHNIS IN THE CAVE OF THE NYMPHS, p. 26

79. CHLOE KISSES DAPHNIS, p. 33 [34]

80. CHLOE PUTS A CHAPLET UPON DAPHNIS' HEAD, p. 42 [46]

81. DAPHNIS TEACHES CHLOE TO PLAY ON THE PIPE, p. 43 [47]

82. DAPHNIS OBSERVES THE SLEEPING CHLOE, p. 44 [48]

83. DAPHNIS DRAWS THE GRASSHOPPER FROM CHLOE'S BOSOM, p. 46 [50]

84. CHLOE CASTING DAPHNIS INTO HER ARMS, p. 53 [58]

85. CHLOE WASHING HER NAKED LIMBS, p. 55 [43]

86. CHLOE BATHING, p. 58 [60]

SECOND BOOK

THIRD BOOK

PAUL VERLAINE: CHANSONS POUR ELLE

TWENTY-FIVE poems by Paul Verlaine with twenty-eight woodcut illustrations by Aristide Maillol. Size of the book 8⅛ x 6. Published by the Editions d'Art Pelletan, Helleu et Sergent, Paris, finished on June 30th, 1939. The edition consists of one hundred and ninety copies: twenty copies on *Japon ancien* numbered 1 to 20; sixty copies on *Montval* numbered 21 to 80; ninety-five copies on *papier du Marais* numbered 81 to 175, and fifteen copies numbered I to XV.

As titles for the woodcuts were selected the first lines of the poems which they illustrate (in accordance with the table of contents of the book).

PUBLIUS VERGILIUS MARO: GEORGICA

THIS publication, planned by Philippe Gonin in Paris, is to be issued in a volume of super-royal format of about 170 pages with illustrations by Aristide Maillol. A prospectus printed in February 1939 announced that the publisher then had in his possession fifteen completed woodcuts and that the artist "sincerely hopes to have the engravings all finished by March. The book is due to come out in April 1939." However, the book has not yet been published, and the woodcuts are probably not even ready. Although a few of these woodcuts may have been executed around 1925 when Count Kessler intended to publish Virgil's *Georgics* after his *Eclogues*, Maillol worked on the illustrations mostly since 1938. In spite of Gonin's announcement that these have been "engraved on wood by the artist himself," Maillol merely drew his compositions on the block and supervised and corrected the engraving.

According to A. Hentzen, *op. cit.*, the *Georgics* were to be illustrated by one hundred woodcuts. But in his announcement Gonin fails to mention the exact number of illustrations. He merely announces a strictly limited edition of eight hundred numbered copies (full Latin text, French translation by Jacques Delille, no foreign edition), printed in black and red, in old Venetian type of the 16th Century, colored headletters, etc. The woodcuts by Maillol are to be erased after printing. Only a few of these woodcuts have as yet been published.

156. PEASANT WITH PLOUGH. First published in *Minotaure* May 1939

157. WOMEN IN THE VINEYARD. First published in *Minotaure*, May 1939

158. WOMEN HARVESTING. First published in *Minotaure*, May 1939

159. CORN. First published in *Minotaure*, May 1939

160. FIGUES. First published in *Minotaure*, May 1939

161. AMANDIER FLEURI. First reproduced in Rewald: *Maillol*, p. 14

Q. HORATIUS FLACCUS: ODES

THIS book planned by Philippe Gonin with numerous woodcuts by Aristide Maillol was to be published after the *Georgics*. The artist has not really started to work on these illustrations, and so far only one woodcut for this book is known.

162. MOTHER AND CHILD. First reproduced in Rewald: *Maillol*, p. 26

1. THE ARTIST'S AUNT

2. HERO AND LEANDER

3. RECLINING WOMAN

4. RECLINING NUDE

5. THE WAVE

6. THE SEA

VERGILIUS MARO: THE ECLOGUES AND GEORGICS IN LATIN AND ENGLISH: VOL. I: THE ECLOGUES

PRINTING OF THE CRANACH PRESS
AT WEIMAR of COUNT HARRY KESSLER
PUBLISHED by EMERY WALKER LONDON

8. LEDA, COVER FOR VIRGIL'S ECLOGUES

P.
VERGILI MARONIS
ECLOGÆ & GEORGICA
LATINE ET GERMANICE
VOLUMEN PRIUS
ECLOGÆ

9. PRESS MARK, TITLE PAGE FOR VIRGIL'S ECLOGUES

(DIE ECLOGEN VERGILS

IN DER URSPRACHE UND DEUTSCH ÜBERSETZT VON RUDOLF ALEXANDER SCHROEDER : MIT ILLUSTRATIONEN

GEZEICHNET UND GESCHNITTEN VON ARISTIDE MAILLOL

10. DAPHNIS PLAYING ON HIS PIPE, FIRST PAGE OF VIRGIL'S ECLOGUES

11. TITYRUS PLAYING ON HIS PIPE

12. GOATS WITH NEWLY BORN TWINS

13. MELIBOEUS AND TITYRUS

14. SHEPHERD CORYDON ARDENTLY IN LOVE

15. A YOUNG GOAT

16. CORYDON SEES HIMSELF IN A POOL

17. THE NYMPHS BRING LILIES IN BASKETS FULL

18. NAIAD ON A DOLPHIN

19. AEGON PUTTING HIS FLOCK IN DAMOETAS' CARE

20. MENALCAS AND DAMOETAS

21. GALATEA AIMS AN APPLE AT DAMOETAS

22. BLOSSOMS

23. LUCINA SMILES ON HER BOY

24. THE EARTH POURS FREELY HER PRESENTS

25. MOPSUS' KIDS AT PASTURE

26. THE WOODLAND NYMPHS WEEPING
THE LOSS OF DAPHNIS

27. A SHEPHERD CARVING VERSE ON
DAPHNIS' FUNERAL MOUND

28. SHEPHERDS AND DRYAD MAIDENS
FILL THE WOODLAND

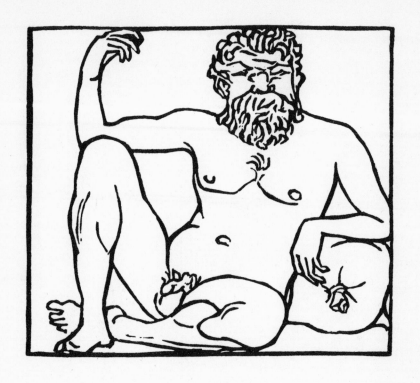

29. SILENUS

30. FAUN AND AEGLE THE LOVELIEST NAIAD

31.　FORESTS　BEGIN　TO　RISE　UP

32. WILD ANIMALS ROAM THE MOUNTAINS

33. HYLAS LEFT BY A STREAM

34. CORYDON AND THYRSIS SINGING
ALTERNATE VERSES

35. MICON OFFERING THE BRANCHING ANTLERS
OF A STAG

36. GALATEA WHITER THAN SWANDOWN

37. GALATEA LOVELIER THAN PALE IVORY

38. A SLEEPING SHEPHERDESS

39. THYRSIS MILKING A GOAT

40. A GIRL UNDER A TREE

41. CUPID

42. MOERIS ON THE ROAD TO TOWN

43. TWO NYMPHS OF THE WOODLANDS

44. TITYRUS AND THE BUCK

45. TITYRUS WITH A GOAT

46. GALATEA IN THE WATER

47. GALATEA DAUGHTER OF NEREUS

48. A NAIAD, NYMPH OF THE SPRINGS

49. PAN OF ARCADY, SILVANUS AND APOLLO

50. HAMADRYADS, GIRLS OF THE WOODLANDS

51. GALLUS HUNTING THE FIERCE WILD BOAR

52. ORNAMENTS, LARGE AND SMALL INITIALS

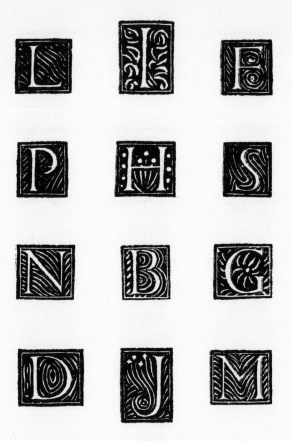

52. ORNAMENTS, LARGE AND SMALL INITIALS

53. A SHEPHERD PLAYING ON HIS PIPE

Q. HORATI FLACCI CARMINUM

Maecenas atavis edite regibus,
O et praesidium et dulce decus meum!
Sunt quos curriculo pulverem Olympicum
Collegisse iuvat, metaque fervidis

54. FAUN AND NYMPH, TITLE PAGE

55. STANDING NUDE, TITLE PAGE

56. INITIAL AND ORNAMENT

57. NUDE WAVING HER HAIR, TITLE PAGE

59. PASIPHAE AND THE WHITE STEER

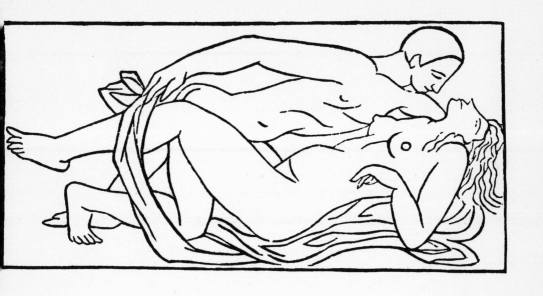

60. ABANDON

61. LOVERS UNDER A TREE

62. DREAMING NUDE

63. LEDA

64. THE KISS

65. LONG CARESS

66. EMBRACE

67. BOY WITH A STAG

68. INITIALS

LES PASTORALES DE
LONGUS OU DAPHNIS
& CHLOÉ • VERSION
D'AMYOT REVUE ET
COMPLÉTÉE PAR
P.·L.COURIER

BOIS ORIGINAUX
D'ARISTIDE MAILLOL

69. CHLOE BATHING, COVER OF THE FRENCH EDITION

LONGUS
DAPHNIS AND CHLOE

70. DAPHNIS AND CHLOE, TITLE PAGE

71. THREE GOATS

72. THREE GOATS

73. TWO NYMPHS DANCING

74. TWO NYMPHS DANCING

75. DAPHNIS AND CHLOE PICKING FLOWERS

76. DAPHNIS PLAYING HIS PIPE FOR CHLOE

77. DAPHNIS PLAYING HIS PIPE FOR CHLOE

78. CHLOE WASHING DAPHNIS IN THE CAVE
OF THE NYMPHS

79. CHLOE KISSES DAPHNIS

80. CHLOE PUTS A CHAPLET UPON DAPHNIS' HEAD

81. DAPHNIS TEACHES CHLOE TO PLAY ON THE PIPE

82. DAPHNIS OBSERVES THE SLEEPING CHLOE

83. DAPHNIS DRAWS THE GRASSHOPPER FROM
CHLOE'S BOSOM

84. CHLOE CASTING DAPHNIS INTO HER ARMS

85. CHLOE WASHING HER NAKED LIMBS

86. CHLOE BATHING

87. THE VINTAGE

88. PHILETAS SPEAKING TO DAPHNIS AND CHLOE

89. THREE GOATS

90. DAPHNIS AND CHLOE SITTING CLOSE TOGETHER

91. DAPHNIS AND CHLOE RUN SMILING TOGETHER

92. DAPHNIS AND CHLOE RUN SMILING TOGETHER

93. DAPHNIS AND CHLOE EMBRACE ONE ANOTHER

94. DAPHNIS AND CHLOE PLAYING

95. DAPHNIS AND CHLOE PLAYING

96. METHYMNAEAN CARRYING CHLOE AWAY

97. DAPHNIS RUSHING INTO THE EMBRACES OF CHLOE

98. DAPHNIS RUSHING INTO THE EMBRACES OF CHLOE

99. DAPHNIS AND CHLOE SACRIFICING
A CROWNED GOAT

100. SYRINX DISAPPEARS IN A GROVE OF REEDS

101. DAPHNIS DRIVING HOME HIS FLOCK

102. DAPHNIS DRIVING HOME HIS FLOCK

103. THREE GOATS RESTING

104. DAPHNIS AND CHLOE REMEMBER THEIR
SWEET CONVERSATION

105. DAPHNIS AND CHLOE IN DRYAS' HOUSE

106. DAPHNIS LIFTS CHLOE UP

107. DAPHNIS LIFTS CHLOE UP

108. LYCAENIUM TEACHES DAPHNIS THE
SECRETS OF LOVE

109. THE ECHO, DAUGHTER OF A NYMPH

110. CHLOE KISSES DAPHNIS

111. DAPHNIS PULLS AN APPLE FOR CHLOE

112. DAPHNIS PUTS THE APPLE INTO CHLOE'S BOSOM

113. DAPHNIS PUTS THE APPLE INTO CHLOE'S BOSOM

114. THREE GOATS

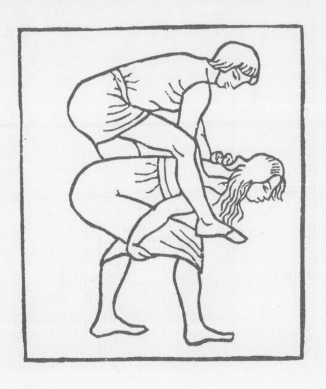

115. DAPHNIS AND CHLOE AT PLAY

116. CHLOE HELPS DAPHNIS WITH HIS GOATS

117. CHLOE HELPS DAPHNIS WITH HIS GOATS

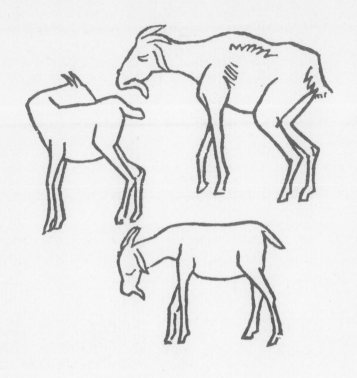

118. THREE GOATS

119. DAPHNIS PLAYS TO HIS GOATS

120. LAMPIS RAVISHING CHLOE AWAY

121. DAPHNIS AND CHLOE

122. CHLOE IS GIVEN TO DAPHNIS

123. DAPHNIS AND CHLOE LYING NAKED TOGETHER

124. DAPHNIS AND CHLOE LYING NAKED TOGETHER

125. DAPHNIS AND CHLOE LYING NAKED TOGETHER

126. CHLOE BATHING IN THE CAVE OF THE NYMPHS

127. INITIALS

Chansons pour Elle

vingt-cinq poèmes de Paul Verlaine
ornés de vingt-huit bois du sculpteur
Aristide Maillol,

tirés à 175 exemplaires que
l'on trouve chez l'artiste et boulevard
Saint-Germain, près la rue de Seine,
à Paris. An mil neuf cent trente neuf.

128. SITTING NUDE, TITLE PAGE

129. TU N'ES PAS DU TOUT VERTUEUSE

130. COMPAGNE SAVOUREUSE ET BONNE

132. OR, MALGRE TA CRUAUTE...

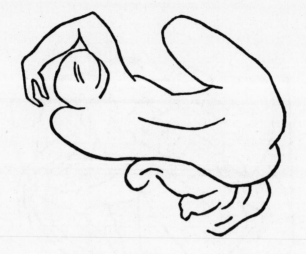

133. JUSQUES AUX PERVERS NONCHALOIRS

134. LA SAISON QUI S'AVANCE

135. JE SUIS PLUS PAUVRE QUE JAMAIS

136. QUE TON AME SOIT BLANCHE OU NOIRE

137. TU M'AS FRAPPE, C'EST RIDICULE

138. L'HORRIBLE NUIT D'INSOMNIE

139. VRAI, NOUS AVONS TROP D'ESPRIT

140. TU BOIS, C'EST HIDEUX...

141. ES-TU BRUNE OU BLONDE?

142. JE NE T'AIME PAS EN TOILETTE

144. L'ÉTÉ NE FUT PAS ADORABLE

146. SI TU LE VEUX BIEN, DIVINE IGNORANTE

147. TON RIRE ECLAIRE MON VIEUX COEUR

149. LORSQUE TU CHERCHES TES PUCES

151. JE N'AI.PAS DE CHANCE EN FEMME

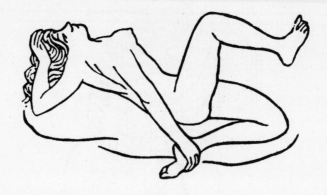

153. JE FUS MYSTIQUE ET JE NE LE SUIS PLUS

154. LEDA

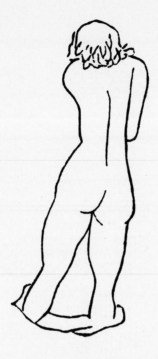

*Achevé d'imprimer
le 30 juin 1939.*

155. STANDING NUDE

156. PEASANT WITH PLOUGH

157. WOMEN IN THE VINEYARD

158. WOMEN HARVESTING